ESSE PURSE MUSEUM PRESENTS

What's Inside?

A Century of Women and Handbags

1900 – 1999

Anita Davis

Nonfiction text by Laura Cartwright Hardy

Fiction text by Rita Henry

Photography by George Chambers, Brandon Markin, and Nancy Nolan

Illustrations by Betsy Davis

Design & Styling by Steven Otis

Little Rock, Arkansas

Copyright © 2018 Anita Davis

Design & Styling by Steven Otis
Edited by Erin Wood
Photographs by George Chambers, Brandon Markin, Nancy Nolan
Illustrations by Betsy Davis
Nonfiction text by Laura Cartwright Hardy
Fiction text by Rita Henry

ISBN: 978-1-944528-86-7
Library of Congress Control Number: 2018958235
Printed in the United States of America

All rights reserved. No part of this book may be reproduced, stored in a retrieval system, or transmitted in any form or by any means, mechanical, electronic, photocopying, recording, or otherwise, without written permission from the publisher, except in the case of reviews. Contact publisher for permission under any circumstances aside from book reviews.

Et Alia Press titles are available at special discounts when purchased in quantity directly from the Press. For details, contact etaliapressbooks@gmail.com or the address below.
Published in the United States of America by:

Et Alia Press
PO Box 7948
Little Rock, AR 72217
etaliapressbooks@gmail.com
etaliapress.com

To my mother and my daughters.

And to the women who found me in dreams:
Through your purses, we hear and see you all.

1510 Main Street
Little Rock, AR 72202
Phone: 501.916.9022
essepursemuseum.com

PREFACE

Strange, but nonetheless there I was, in Little Rock, Arkansas, sitting atop a crate full of purses I'd collected over more than thirty years. The collection's return in 2011 from a professionally curated five-year nationwide traveling exhibition to small history museums from Concord, Massachusetts, to Seattle, Washington, loomed as large as the container. The excitement of a successful tour extended for a second run to more museums was through. Documenting the purses' travels and hearing stories of how they'd mattered to people along their way had filled me with pride and energy.

Opening the crate, I encountered the purses once more like old friends. I reunited with the wicker bust of a woman from a New York antique market, the Ingber black wool safety pin purse that I'd found in central Arkansas, and a leather box bag from my own mother's closet in Murfreesboro, Arkansas (which took me back to childhood days when I swooned over it as I imagined the lives of the cast bronze Dutch girl and boy mounted to its exterior). Since I hadn't seen most of the purses in several years, it was hard not to while away the hours with nostalgia. Not knowing exactly what to do with the purses, I left them in their storage area and locked the door. Perhaps they had served their purpose. Imagining it all coming to an end, I couldn't help but feel deflated.

As I slept over the next few weeks, dreams came strong and vividly painted. Women came to me in flashes, their faces appearing one after another after another like rolling pictures. She, her, she, her, she, her . . . more and more and more women, faces I'd never seen in my life. In the gazes of all these women, I became locked. Not exactly a haunting, but they wouldn't leave me alone. Women, always more women, stirring me, urging me. *To do what?*

When they finally answered, they whispered into my ear as one: *We have more stories to tell*. And then it clicked. The purses had belonged to these women. No longer an end, the women who streamed through my dreams spoke of a new beginning.

While exploring what to do next, I found and bought a building on Main Street in Little Rock, one built in 1948 with a history of its own. It seemed a good fit for the collection, but what might that mean? As I considered, I assembled a new creative team to help me reconfigure the traveling exhibit for a permanent space.

As we worked, we realized we were actually curating a women's history museum, one that tells the story of the American woman from 1900 to 1999 through her constantly changing purses and the items she carried in them. We would call it ESSE, Latin for "to be." As a purse holds the identity of each woman and is a symbolic container for the feminine, the museum would house the purses and share with the world how countless women's identities

Leather Box Purse

Brass fittings with brass
Dutch boy and girl figures

and the contents of their purses were shaped by the forces at work during the eras in which they lived. Along with photographs of women holding their purses and decade copy to provide historical context, each display case was developing as a mini history lesson, with a dose of fashion.

As the museum's vision became clear, I also began to value the importance not only of sharing the stories of women past, but of supporting contemporary women whose lives intersect with the purse. The ESSE Store was born, and is stocked with a rotating mix of mindfully curated vintage and new, elegant and cheeky, practical and whimsical, so ideally there is something for every woman on every occasion at a price that is comfortable for her pocketbook. The inventory is selected with an eye toward fair trade, one-of-a-kind, cultivation of artistry, and fostering the power of the sacred feminine. It is a distinct honor to see customers leave the store with purses that will be at their sides or the sides of their chosen recipient as they conduct their daily business, nurture their dreams, and unlock their own feminine power.

As I walk through ESSE Museum & Store on the eve of its 5th birthday in its permanent location, I continue to believe in the radical importance of thinking about the women who owned each and every purse inside. Through their purses, I see and hear them all. It is emboldening to witness others seeing and hearing them too. Through our foremothers, we open a new relationship with our own feminine. By witnessing their acts of courage, we gain courage of our own to discover what it is we came into this world to do and to serve our own highest purposes.

While we more commonly think of changes for women being brought about by famous names whose stories are more accessible, I think of the women who owned these purses as our unnamed heroines. It is delightful to know that these women can now live together at ESSE, alive in their purse striking a visitor's fancy, respected in being wondered about, new life breathed into them through the curiosity of another—that other perhaps me or you. What a fun way to spend hours, thinking of the ordinary activities of their daily lives, within reach to us all through their purses: women tucking in business cards that will lead to their first jobs, hiding birth control pills from their mothers, bribing their children with chocolates, medicating themselves and loved ones through illnesses, powdering their noses, putting on bright new lipsticks, storing curlers they forgot to remove from their hair while rushing off to work, stashing portable breast pumps, stowing temporarily hats they'll wear to march for the rights of all women. Women evolving through the decades, carrying so much on our shoulders.

On behalf of the women who first appeared in my dreams and now accompany me in my daily waking life at ESSE, I hope this book connects you to a purse or a woman who strikes your fancy as you consider *What's Inside*. This is just a beginning. We all have many more stories to share.

—Anita Davis
Founder, ESSE Museum & Store

INTRODUCTION

The purse holds power.

Some husbands and sons so fear purses that they'd rather bring them to their wives or mothers than reach inside to find the car keys; to do otherwise would be an intrusion into a sacred, feminine space, which might be eerie, and maybe a little threatening.

When we seek *What's Inside* the purse of another, perhaps there is a breach. Nonetheless, there are mother lodes to discover, extraordinary riches within. The complexities of a woman cannot be fully explained or defined through the contents of her purse, but hints about her identity abound in the depths of her bag and what she chooses to carry. If a woman goes missing and her purse remains behind, everyone knows something bad has happened, or she wants to disappear, because no woman in a good place would willingly lose her handbag. (Sharp detectives turn to purses for clues and to get a feel for the woman herself in missing persons and murder cases. That's how revealing handbags can be.) If a thief grabs her bag, she won't let go easily. Steal a woman's purse and you've stolen a piece of her.

Just as a purse is more than a purse, ESSE Museum & Store is more than a museum. Within its walls, purses and contents reveal much about the women of each decade and their evolving positions in the public sphere. Through it, we honor the women who came before us, offering a much-needed reminder of the strength and courage of usually unsung heroines. We at ESSE love to see the joyful smiles and wistful tears of our visitors as they wander through purse-sized monuments and are reminded of their own mothers, grandmothers, sisters, aunts, and other women who have played important roles in their lives. Some visitors return to generously gift a special purse or even a collection—often in honor or memory of a woman close to their hearts. We are extraordinarily grateful for their donations. As each of us are reminded of these women, we celebrate our collective female relatives who, through acts small and large throughout the 20th century, forged the way for contemporary American women. These women, these backbones of America, are the essence of ESSE.

Out of unbounded reverence for women past, present, and future, we have assembled this volume as another tender offering of thanks. Through it, we intend to extend the museum experience, further exploring concepts of art, history, and the feminine. The book's decade by decade peek inside the purse, like the museum, is the vision of Anita Davis, conductor of collaborative efforts.

Each decade opens with a photographed exterior view of a quintessential handbag of the era before its contents are spilled for consideration. These pages were curated and styled by ESSE Art Director, Steven Otis, and are illuminated by the micro-histories of lifelong journalist Laura Cartwright Hardy. Hardy's words also grace the display case plaques at ESSE, providing historical grounding for the purses and ephemera contained within as they do in this book. Readers will next encounter the vibrant illustrations of Betsy Davis, daughter of ESSE founder Anita Davis. These works provide an opportunity to visually muse on women's personalities and identities within the context of their era. Betsy Davis' illustrations are paired with stories by Rita Henry, whose historically-informed fictions contemplate what might have happened beyond the slices of life captured in colored pencil. Altogether, these four mediums infuse the decades not only with what was, but with what very well *might have been*, venerating the stories of all women as they beg us to restore them to life through our imaginings, whether or not we are able to know the precise circumstances of their lives.

As you read, we hope you will find yourself dreaming. Perhaps, as you wander through an estate sale, an auntie's closet, or a vintage store, you will be beckoned to fathom the story of the woman or women who carried a purse you encounter there—to ponder what may have been her style, habits, secrets, fears, and joys. And most of all, as you read and contemplate, we hope you have fun asking *What's Inside?*

1900s

In the early years of the 20th century, not much changed outwardly for women. The fashions of the late 1800s died hard, which was fitting for such stiff and modest attire. In most homes, the attitudes that gave rise to corset and bustle still bound the woman of the house to her husband, making her more property than partner. But some women felt stirrings of the winds of change the new century would bring and began claiming the right to leave the house unaccompanied to socialize with friends, or attend lectures or political gatherings. In some cases, blustering men didn't know what had hit them, but the more acquiescent just went with the flow.

A wealthy woman—who charged purchases to her husband's account and had no need for cash, was too high-class for cosmetics, and didn't need keys since a maid or butler waited at home to open her door—could still get by sans purse, or with a delicate little thing carried more for effect than effectiveness. But the average woman found she needed something substantial enough to carry her essential items of daily life as she began spending more time away from home pursuing her favorite activities.

Since a working woman didn't have the luxury of staying home on "those days," not only did she need to carry her lunch, keys, and coin purse, but at that time of the month, she also had to tote her cumbersome, well, *you know*. And probably a tin of a new over-the-counter medicine called "aspirin" for her unmentionable pain, as well as her sore feet and hands.

As the decade progressed, practicality reigned, and what we know as the modern handbag was born. Sturdy, reinforced, almost suitcase-like carryalls—think Mary Poppins minus the magic—became the norm for day, and shimmering mesh bags became the must-have for evenings out, at least for those who could afford them.

Savvy purse makers paid attention, and satchel-like purses became more sophisticated to fit women's changing needs. Soon, bags were designed for particular occasions with clever interior compartments for specific items. Along with traditionally feminine accessories—handkerchief, fan, calling cards, and smelling salts (because one never knew when a lady might have a fainting spell, or feint one for effect)—a woman's bag might contain her bankbook, change purse, notepad, tiny pencil, and house key.

Progress!

Original Design
Hand-tooled leather bag

Canteen-Shaped Purse
Suede with celluloid

Mary Grace Hollins

Baltimore, Maryland

1900 – 1909

"Hello, it is a pleasure to meet you. I am Mrs. John Cumberland Hollins. Mary Grace Hollins. You may have heard of the Hollinses? The family has been in Baltimore for over a century.

"And this child to my right is Rebecca, our daughter, who is looking for her lost Teddy Bear. These popular Teddy Bears, as the advertisement says, are "the best plaything ever invented . . . the most sensible and serviceable." Oh, yes, and here is dear Cora, our cat.

"Our governess, Isabella, takes care of Rebecca's outdoor activities when I am away from the house. Wholesome games are lined up in the playground to exercise her mind and body.

"There are several places to visit today, from Federal Hill almost to the Harbor. I understand you'll accompany me on my outing? Shopping is work, you know. I would like to purchase a book to read to Rebecca. Maybe L. Frank Baum's *The Wizard of Oz*. She certainly has enjoyed *The Tale of Peter Rabbit*. Children must be read to daily.

"Since it will soon be the sociable season, I will need a book to discuss. I recently read *Rebecca of Sunnybrook Farm*: "The soul grows into lovely habits as easily as into ugly ones." A nice thought. For something challenging, I have heard much of Upton Sinclair's *The Jungle* . . . very political. Perhaps I will choose it, or maybe another.

"Last week, I shopped for purses. Asked questions and negotiated a bit. I think it's time to purchase. I need an evening bag for the opera. I found a beautiful Irish crochet handbag with such delicate lace, and several silver chatelaine bags with mesh and bead. Some have such captivating raised flowers and birds and cherubs. We should also look at the leather handbags, the ones that strap to the belt and help free the hands.

"This purse with a security clasp is perfect for our outing. Let me check inside. Did the maid put in our family calling cards with the apron edges? We might have time to drop a card by the new banker's residence for the lady of the house. I see the lavender smelling salts, the silk and linen handkerchief. There is the calling card case! Good.

"I'd love to browse the music counter at the department store. What do you think of the ragtime tunes? There is some debate over the quality of the pieces, yet I heard "The Entertainer" and it was impressive. I am debating what music to perform for the ladies when they visit. Maybe "Toyland," or a romantic piece by Chopin. My parents sent me to St. Timothy's girls' school, which was first class, but what I would have given to be a student at the Peabody Conservatory of Music! Some women are receiving college degrees. The Maryland Women's Suffrage Association even helped women become a part of the Johns Hopkins Medical School. Women studying beyond a dash of literature, history, and art. Someday women may even vote! With my household, my social calendar, and the church Women's Auxiliary, I strain to find time for more than the classics and parlor entertainment.

"Let's be on our way. Life is moving fast. My husband informed me this morning he will purchase a Ford Model T, so perhaps we can go for a ride on our next excursion!"

1910s

Women's baby steps toward emancipation in the dawning years of the new century gave way to full-on teen spirit and sass in the next decade, with women asserting themselves more and more, often standing up to their husbands and other men in charge. The teen decade's demonstrations and demands to be taken seriously would gain American women the federal right to vote in 1920.

Oddly, for a bit, purses moved to the forefront of the battleground.

Some suffragists, in their demand for equal rights with men, argued for the right to have pockets in their clothes; to them, handbags were oppressive accessories for oppressed women, and having to carry one across the forearm or in the hand limited physical freedom (though they could be used quite effectively to whack a bellicose counter-protestor, should the need arise). But more women had grown to love pocketbooks for the convenience they offered and the independence they represented. A "Ban the bag!" movement bombed.

The bombs and horrors of the war in Europe that erupted in 1914 drew America into the conflict in 1917. At home, World War I brought an explosion of opportunities and responsibilities for some

women, who became heads of households as their husbands marched off to war. Other women marched off to the workplace for the first time in their lives to replace the missing men. And the shortage of domestic help that arose from women entering the workforce brought changes in fashion and purses.

Clothing grew simpler: With no one to help draw a corset tight or fasten rows of tiny buttons, women demanded simpler designs. Conversely, purses grew more complex, as women wanted not only more options in serviceable bags to make life easier, but more styles of handbags to suit more purposes. Art Nouveau hand-tooling on leather bags became de rigueur. Small purses with wrist straps suited some women for finer occasions, and the shimmery mesh bag of earlier years continued to flourish, staying in vogue well into the 1930s.

Handbags soon had compartments to hold now-acceptable cosmetics, as well as money, cards, stamps, and more. Purse accessories also became popular: manicure cases, checkbook cases, and compacts.

As the country outgrew the teen years, the pocketbook matured from novelty to necessity. And the diversity and range of purses available meant that every woman, from every level of society, would carry a bag.

Handmade Reticule
Tatting with drawstring closure and pompon trim

Handmade Brocade Purse
Asian design with herringbone braided metallic trim

Mrs. Helen Hanna Tucker and Mrs. Evelyn Selden McLean

Washington, D.C.
1910 – 1919

March 1913.

We find Mrs. Helen Hanna Tucker and Mrs. Evelyn Selden McLean visiting in Farragut Square Park near Dupont Circle in Washington, D.C. Helen has the silver beaded chatelaine purse. Evelyn carries a Mandalian mesh purse.

Helen and Evelyn met in the Junior League of Washington. Now both are married with children and live on the same block of row houses. Together they attend the Washington Readers' Club as well as the same sewing circle. They volunteer in the community, working to better the welfare of children and those without means. Their households each include a nurse and a maid to care for the young children. Having these servants allows Helen and Evelyn time to participate in the community and manage the day-to-day shopping.

Since her husband had finished reading them first, Helen brings several evening and morning papers to the park bench. Evelyn anxiously waits to read the current events in Washington. The two are taking time to study and discuss recent news of great significance.

Helen: "John said he saw Red Cross ambulances. I considered walking the few blocks to the parade, but John, with his position on the court, did not feel comfortable. He hesitates to support women voting. With all the people, I don't think anyone would have noticed. He did attend the inauguration."

Evelyn: "A parade to demand women's right to vote. What a sight it must have been! What do the newspapers say?"

Helen: "Woodrow Wilson was arriving at the railroad station only a few blocks away. The suffrage parade and the inauguration almost collided! The headlines say, 'INAUGURAL THRONGS CHEER SUFFRAGE PARADE,' and 'ARRIVAL OF WILSON EAGERLY AWAITED BY 250,000 VISITORS.' Look at these photographs. I've never seen so many people."

Evelyn: "What a beautiful picture. A woman in a white gown on a white horse!"

Helen: "It says, 'Inez Milholland Boissevain was wearing a white cape and seated on a white horse.' She is a Washington lawyer and led the parade down Pennsylvania Avenue. Behind her were nine bands, four mounted brigades, three heralds, twenty-four floats, and more than 5,000 marchers. There were people in costumes representing countries of the world where women can vote. Evelyn, you look in the evening home edition."

Evelyn: "Here it shows delegations from five states in golden chariots. There was a Liberty Bell float and women marched in groups determined by their occupation. Jeannette Rankin, the lady representative from Montana, marched. So did Helen Keller. And, of course, Alice Paul."

Helen: "This paper lists the groups: nurses, farmers, homemakers, doctors, librarians, and even a section of male supporters of women's suffrage. They hope Woodrow Wilson will support an amendment for women's right to vote . . . and pass it before he leaves office."

Evelyn: "Listen to this: 'A mob hurts 300 suffragists. Men in town for the following day's inauguration surged into the street, making it almost impossible for the marchers to pass. Women were jeered, tripped, grabbed, and shoved, and many heard indecent epithets and barnyard conversation.' It was said the police seemed to enjoy all the jokes."

Helen: "The ambulances John saw must have been for the parade marchers!"

Evelyn: "Charles said after reading the paper that most women don't want to vote. He said it was unkind to add the burdens of government to women's busy schedules of duties to the church, society, and charity."

Helen: "Well, Susan B. Anthony said women lack power because they lack money. We can't have a bank account without a husband. Miss Anthony carried change in an alligator purse as a symbol of her financial independence."

Evelyn: "We need new purses, even if we have to buy on account. Symbolic purses!"

Helen: "The Palais Royal advertisement has so many things. Skating costumes, opera bags, fans, and silk and beaded bags . . . so many shapes and colors! Lovely silk bags, veiled with gold and metal laces. $2.00 to $21.00 each."

Evelyn: "Maybe our displays of financial independence could be silk bags with ostrich feather fans inside. Would Susan B. Anthony approve?"

1920s

As the 1920s roared to life, American women had their first "hear me roar" movement. Soon after the liberation of winning the right to vote nationwide, women decided the time had come to break free from the oppressive shackles of fashion that carried over from the previous century. For thoroughly modern and daring gals, that meant discarding restrictive undergarments, deciding short skirts were the bee's knees, and—gasp—bobbing their hair.

Though some women were scandalized by the new looks and behavior, preferring more modest dress and ladylike decorum, others openly embraced the flapper lifestyle by smoking, drinking, and dancing the night away. But women all along the spectrum of style agreed on one thing: The purse had become a staple of every put-together woman's wardrobe.

Staple didn't mean staid in the Roaring Twenties, though, and purses took on a new incarnation as fashion showpiece. A geometric Art Deco evening bag—adorned with glitter, embroidery, beading, or even feathers—could be a showstopper. Since all women now needed at least one, purses were in high demand at every price point; catalogs like Sears & Roebuck offered wide varieties at reasonable costs, so even the average woman could buy an array of handbags in bright modernist designs and new materials, like patent leather.

New materials included ever-so-modern and versatile plastics, which opened the purse to a new world of novelty shapes and designs, particularly for the clutch, the "it" bag of the decade. (Bakelite, of course, was the gold standard for plastic purses.) Streamlined to express the exhilarating pace of modern life, the clutch was totally impractical for everyday use—too small to carry anything of significance, easily dropped and, by putting one arm out of action to "clutch" it to the body, physically restricting.

But, oh, were they chic!

The thoroughly modern woman thought nothing of touching up her face in public, and an attractive purse and accessories made a touch-up a glamourous thing to do. Beautiful enameled or bejeweled compacts and lipstick cases quickly became must-haves. Handbag designers were just as quick to cash in on this new need to carry cosmetics. Many purses had pockets for cosmetics, a mirror, a perfume vial, and a cigarette case and lighter, so all could be stowed in their proper places.

The merry-go-round 1920s were wild until the economy crashed in 1929, ruining a decade-long cocktail party. But what a liberating ride they'd been.

Beaded Evening Purse
with kiss lock closure

Foldover Vanity Purse
Rhombus shaped with Bakelite handle and exterior compact

Barbara and Colleen

Cincinnati, Ohio

1920 – 1929

On work days, Barbara and Colleen, two young women of Cincinnati, "the Queen City," stroll down Vine Street alongside other women on their way to jobs as clerks, bookkeepers, and waitresses. They are educated flappers employed as sales clerks at Pogue's, a seven-story dry goods store at 4th and Race Streets downtown. After work, they might meet a date at a hidden speakeasy to drink bootleg cocktails and smoke cigarettes.

This late spring Saturday morning, Barbara picks up Colleen in her new "breezer" convertible and they drive to the Ohio River Launch Club. This pleasure boating experience with Buster, the dog, is a causal weekend affair, yet they both dress well. Barbara steers the leased boat in her rayon chenille crepe dress ($9.95). Colleen, holding onto Buster, brings with her a pink beaded handbag ($1.25), and a close-fitting cloche, embellished with satin ribbon ($1.85).

Colleen: "Atta girl, Barbara. This boat ride is unreal. And you are so dolled up! You look like Joan Crawford with your scarf rolled."

Barbara: "This boating is much better than ankling it. Charlie, the bell bottom on the dock, told us to stay near the shoreline."

Colleen: "I heard they water ski in Minnesota. 'If you could ski on snow, you could ski on water.' I can't do either!"

Barbara: "That sounds on the level. You and Buster don't panic—there are a few waves ahead. We'll head west and all will be copacetic."

Colleen: "Can we dock downtown? We could buy the sheet music to 'Sweet Georgia Brown.' And maybe we can listen to the radio at the music counter. WLW!"

Barbara: "My mother stood in line for hours to buy a Roger's receiver. Now she listens to the WLW morning devotion, YMCA exercises, and baseball."

Colleen: "I heard a keen violin piece on WLW during the eclipse in January. In the darkness, the sound was crystal clear."

Barbara: "You can't do the Charleston or Black Bottom to a violin piece, though."

Colleen: "After studying church music, you are just a floorflusher looking for a sharpshooter . . . any handsome man who can dance!"

Barbara: "Maybe we should put on the ritz this weekend and go to Cosmopolitan Hall. I have the password."

Colleen: "I need something new to wear. Did you see the new handbags at Pogue's? I stood on my dogs all day at work, but found my way to the new handbags. One is imported with enameled mesh black-and-white flowers, and it can hold lipstick, powder, gloves, and cash. Maybe I could put it on layaway."

Barbara: "Maybe a sugar daddy can buy you that swanky evening bag."

Colleen: "I can get my own money. Look, I have a sawbuck in my purse next to Buster. Oops! Better not rock the boat."

Barbara: "Aww, applesauce! You have ten dollars? Then you can buy me a handbag with a mirror. Oh, the sunski is too bright today to boat!"

Colleen: "Poor little bunny. You need one strong shot of brown plaid from the Cosmopolitan Hall. Or better yet, the Hotel Sinton's 'champagne grape juice.' Couldn't get you plastered if you drank a hundred!"

Barbara: "Right now, this tomato could handle some of that noodle juice . . . tea! Buster can ride in the back of the breezer and enjoy the wind flapping his ears. Let's head to shore and get a wiggle on."

1930s

Except for a minority of the fabulously wealthy who were able to maintain the high life, the 1930s brought gloom, drudgery, and an exercise in getting by—a hard row to hoe, especially after the glitz and glibness of the previous decade. After the initial shock of the crash of '29 wore off, reality set in, and the real world brought the lean, tough years of the Great Depression and the Dust Bowl of the Great Plains. Fashion for most reflected that somber and sober reality.

But movies remained fairly affordable and offered an escape from the hardness and hardship of daily life. Women could get doses of the deluxe life in darkened theaters without denting their pocketbooks too badly. From the big screen, they could also take in tips on spicing things up via hairdos, makeup, plucked eyebrows, and nail polish—inexpensive ways to add pizzazz.

Gone were glamour and the days of new dresses for each season; clothes were expected to wear well and be simple enough to last several years without looking too dated. Accessories, though, were another story for those with a modicum of spending money. A matching purse and shoes, plus costume jewelry, could jazz things up for minimal expense, especially since the Depression drove manufacturers to less-expensive and faux materials.

Plastic purses in sleek, rounded shapes paired with makeup cases of plastic—carved or molded and set with paste—could make a gal feel special. Cute handbags made of inexpensive wooden beads fit many budgets, too. Women held tightly to the clutch well into the 1930s.

Art Deco themes and styles remained popular throughout the decade (though perhaps only in dreams), but as the Depression dragged on and grim circumstances prevailed, purses began to reflect a new seriousness; form, function, and sturdiness grew in importance, and women turned to the idea of owning just one "good" handbag.

By the later '30s, as financial woes eased, dress began to take on a military style, as photos and newsreels of the war in Europe became embedded in the American psyche. The clutch finally fell from favor, and the shoulder strap, slung over sturdy padded shoulders, moved to the fashion forefront. Women would need something substantial to carry them through the next few years.

Celluloid Minaudière
with Bakelite

Czech Wooden Beaded Purse
with kiss lock closure

Patricia Carol Bullitt

Louisville, Kentucky
1930 – 1939

"My name is Patricia Carol Bullitt from Louisville, Kentucky, the River City. Yes, I heard it first on the radio. They were reading headline bulletins: 'Earhart Plane Lost at Sea,' 'Radio Men Hear Earhart Voice Faintly,' 'SOS from Amelia,' '58 Planes to Hunt Amelia.' It was July 2 when Amelia Earhart was lost. She was my hero. When I was very young, I first heard that 'The Angel of the Air,' Amelia, flew in Powder Puff Derbies and had a plane called Friendship. She said, 'Adventure is worthwhile in itself.' It all seemed so inspiring. After setting new records for altitude, speed, and solo flights crossing oceans, this brave woman was flying around the world!

"Before Christmas, and before the flood changed everything, I was in downtown Louisville at the Rialto to see *After the Thin Man*. Amelia was shown in a newsreel at the Lockheed factory with her airplane, the Electra. In May (about the time Churchill Downs reopened after the flood), I read that Amelia flew the Electra in her last flight. She was attempting to go around the Equator. My mother thinks of Amelia Earhart as just a tomboy in men's aviator clothes. I think of her as womanly—elegant, tall, and slim in the latest fashions. I have always admired her for more than that, of course.

When she needed money to buy a better airplane, she began making clothes at home just like the rest of us, except she sold her clothes at Macy's. My mother showed me an advertisement for an Amelia Earhart dress made of parachute silk with buttons crafted from airplane nuts and bolts. Since it was during hard times economically, her clothes didn't sell well, so she quit making them. Too bad women fix up by just adding a new purse to an old dress or she might have been able to keep designing. Instead, my hero has disappeared.

"I can surely understand why Amelia wanted to fly and be above it all with the stars and moon. This year, 1937, all of us in Louisville would rather have been in an airplane than on Earth. While President Roosevelt was in the middle of his second inauguration, it was so bad in Kentucky that

LIFE magazine sent a photographer to show America the flooding, the tent villages, and the lines at the soup kitchens. Our city, seventy percent underwater, was featured in the February 15th issue.

"It never stopped raining during January, but we didn't expect the constant sogginess to develop into water rushing everywhere. The Ohio River was twenty-four miles wide in some places. I continued to work at the University of Louisville until we lost heat and water. In January, we listened to KHAS on the crystal radio sets and tried to keep warm. The radio announcer—they say he was dangling from a telephone pole—directed a rescue boat to our area so we didn't have to cross the bridge they made from whiskey barrels. I evacuated with my parents to the southwest highlands.

"There was a great fire during the flood. The rain was cold and it even snowed. There was fear of typhoid. Store merchandise was taken by the authorities for emergency use. Everything was being rationed. When the flood water receded, it smelled terrible. Many areas of town were restricted and we needed a pass to return home. I was so glad I had my Ward's wool coat and my Oxford shoes. I could have used one of those English military rain coats and BF Goodrich boots. I was separated from my fiancé, Samuel Walker, for a month. Although the dentistry school didn't entirely close, he left school to work with the government emergency relief. Our wedding is now delayed until the city is stabilized.

"During the flood, Samuel traveled to North Carolina and brought us back a newspaper with an article tracking Amelia Earhart's last flight. He thought the gap in Amelia's teeth ruined her pretty face. I imagined that was just because he was studying dentistry, but I heard Amelia's husband thought the same, and rumors circulated that her husband had told her to smile with her mouth closed. In the last photograph I saw of Amelia, she was smiling with mouth closed, standing next to her airplane. I prefer to imagine her with her teeth showing. She had a monogrammed Gladstone bag along with her aviator's wear. Maybe they will find her and her navigator on an uncharted island. I hope the ocean didn't take Amelia like the river took people here in the Louisville flood. 1937 is turning out to be a tragic year."

1940s

Even before the United States joined the Allies in World War II, the War's effects were felt in America, as the pace quickened and employment rose. After the bombs hit Pearl Harbor on December 7, 1941, the date FDR predicted would "live in infamy," hell broke loose on the islands, and the U.S. would never be the same. The pace of life took on a new urgency after the lethargy of the Depression, and fashion retreated to the back burner as wartime rationing affected every aspect of life.

As men once more marched off to war, women marched back to the forefront of offices and industry, and their clothing and purses quickly adapted to fit their new status as working women. Slacks required by factory jobs became fashionable, along with military-like shoulder pads and muted colors adopted in deference to the seriousness of war. These stood in sharp contrast to the shorter skirts (which saved on fabric) and shoulder-length hair (fewer trips to the beauty shop) of the war years.

Austerity drove fashion, but women didn't seem to mind. Short skirts as patriotic duty added a fun element to USO parties, and accessories, whether inexpensively bought or homemade, became festive accent pieces for humbler clothes.

One indispensable accessory was heavily influenced by WWII. Leather purses became unaffordable for many (and a bit unpatriotic, as leather was diverted to the military for boots and gear). But purses

in other materials grew larger and more practical to accommodate self-sufficient women with can-do attitudes. The freedom of movement that came with slacks and shorter skirts let women walk quickly and confidently, and large tote bags loaded with essentials (ration books, coupons, identity cards, sewing kits, and hairnets) tossed over a shoulder added to the effect.

Some women had their good leather handbags remodeled; others made or mended their own purses. Fabric bags, especially in the patriotic hues of red, white, and blue, modestly bedazzled a drab outfit. Improvements in plastics, synthetics, and imitation patent leather made new bags snazzy but affordable.

At the War's end, men came home, women were sent (or happily went) home to resume their previous roles, and French designer Christian Dior's "New Look" of 1947 brought elegance and femininity back into full bloom. Long, full skirts, fitted bodices, high heels, and ladylike hats required sleek, elegant clutch purses for balance, and shoulder bags became unpopular reminders of war.

This look would flower for years.

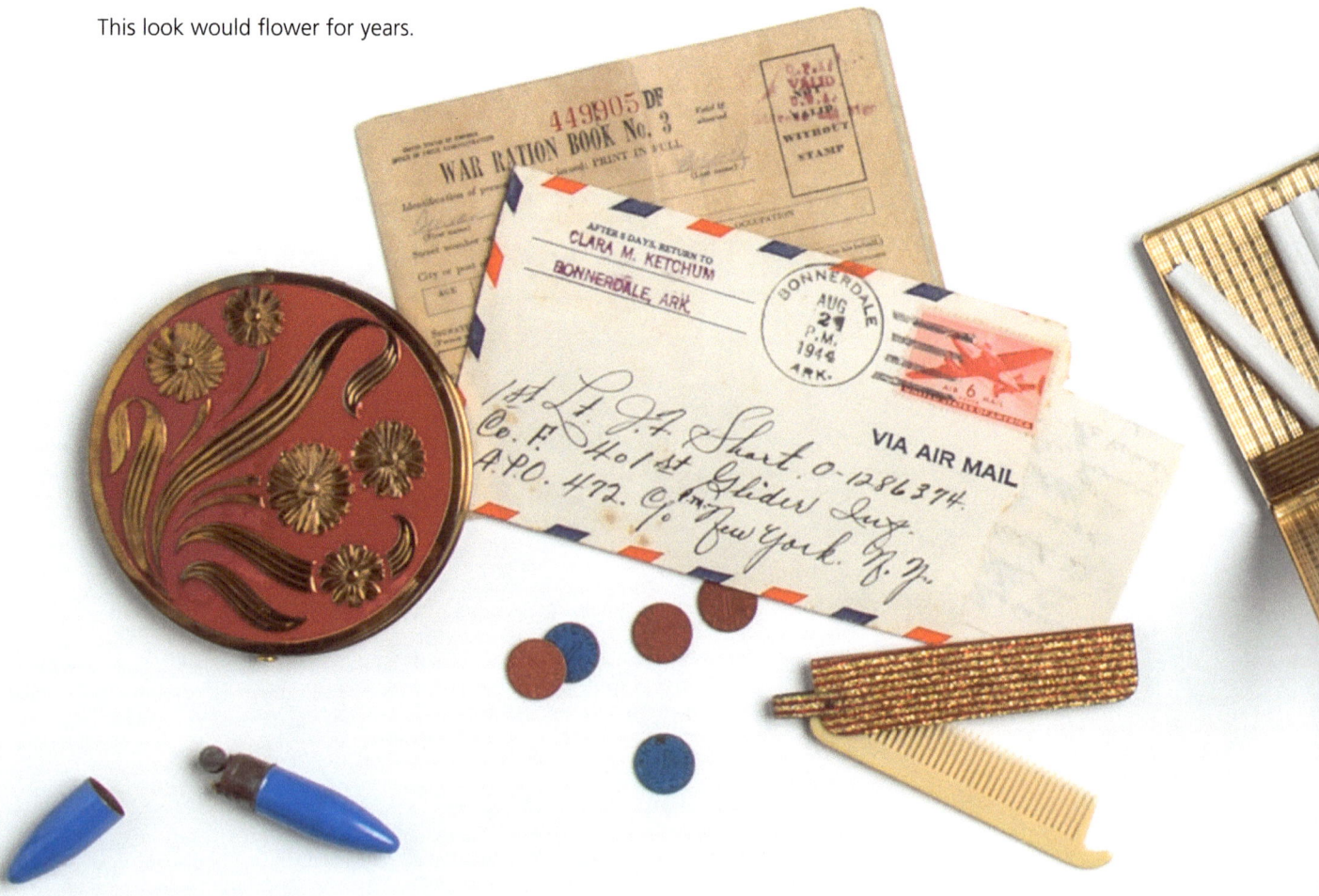

Wrist Purse

Alligator embossed
green vinyl

Suede Frame Bag
with Bakelite handle and kiss lock closure

Annie, Marian, and Catherine

St. Louis, Missouri
1940 – 1949

Annie, Marian, and Catherine wait for the choir processional on Palm Sunday at the Antioch Baptist Church in the Ville neighborhood of St. Louis. These young women attended church and school together almost all their lives. Sumner High School, a few blocks away, is their alma mater. With high school graduation a year before, this church service marks an unofficial reunion for the three. This week in 1941, the march down the center aisle of the church includes the choir members singing, carrying palm branches, and leading the congregation members into the sanctuary. The processional is about to begin.
"Sing Hosanna to the chosen one."

Annie, with a new straw hat, borrowed her mother's beaded handbag, skirt, and jacket and dressed them up with a new blouse and broach. She is training at the Homer G. Phillips Hospital to become a nurse. She plans to tell her friends today that she wants to join the Cadet Nurse Corps. Unlike most of the world, the United States isn't officially at war, but the government is opening up a few opportunities to women like Annie. It helps that she has some training already. In exchange for service to her country, Annie will receive the best on-the-job education anywhere, plus room and board, uniforms, and pay.

Marian wears a sombrero hat and veil, along with a new clutch purse, necklace, and bracelet. Like her mother before her, Marian attends beauty school. Her mother graduated from Annie Malone's Poro College of Beauty Culture and owns a beauty salon, Ladies of Distinction. Marian is newly engaged to Robert Tibbs. Her friends didn't seem to notice, but her ring is very thin since metals are becoming more scarce and expensive. Finding no silk due to the war, Marian made her Sunday dress from a Simplicity pattern with sturdier material and a shorter skirt so as to use less fabric.

Catherine wears a corsage which she created fresh today from her garden. She thought it a nice touch since the three women have an appointment later for a group portrait. The photography studio—the same one that shot the friends' 1939 prom portraits—uses the latest in backdrop trends of velvet curtains and pastoral scenes. Catherine is

studying at Stowe's Teachers College with a particular interest in English. She dresses up today with a felt sombrero tilt hat, white gloves, and soft curled hair.

The church organ music begins to swell and the choir, cloaked in purple robes, assembles at the church's front doors. As these friends enjoy this church ritual they know so well, they cannot imagine how their lives will change in the coming year. With the December 7th Japanese attack on Pearl Harbor and the United States' declaration of war, they will find themselves listening and waiting. The three women will gather round the Philco radio at Catherine's home as Roosevelt in his 1942 State of the Union Address says, "This production of ours in the United States must be raised far above present levels, even though it will mean the dislocation of the lives and occupations of millions of our own people." Roosevelt's words will hold true.

Marian will become the wife of Robert Tibbs three days before he leaves for the U.S. Marine Corps in 1942. She will work two jobs, the beauty shop and the daycare at Curtiss-Wright Aircraft Factory. After serving with distinction, Robert will perish on a beach in Saipan, earning a Purple Heart. Marian will raise their son alone.

Catherine will continue her college classes during the day and work nights at a factory supplying troops with uniforms and footwear. She will marry a college classmate, Wally Evans. While stationed in the Southwest Pacific under the command of General Douglas MacArthur, he will be one of the many Army Air Force pilots killed in action.

Annie will become an Army nurse in England caring for German POWs. When she can, she will correspond with her Homefront friends. Everyday life in England and America is oriented toward victory in the War. Everything from metal and leather to sugar and fabric is rationed. Catherine and Marian will get together when they can and sew their own drawstring purses from small pieces of fabric. They will crochet a beautiful handbag with an old dress zipper and patchwork satin lining and mail it to Annie in England. Several months later, Annie will write to thank them and explain, "Even in the middle of war, I must remember that they say nursing is the alleviation of suffering through diagnosis and treatment . . . and the care of individuals, families, communities, and populations."

But before any of this, they are just three lifelong friends attending church, on their way to cast in celluloid a day in their lives together on the verge of their next adventures.

1950s

After their relative freedom to work and take charge at home during WWII, some women bristled at being sent back to domesticity, but by and large, women were thrilled to have their men back and were happy to return home. Post-war prosperity and the baby boom birthed a renewed emphasis on the roles of happy homemaker and mother for most women in the 1950s, roles that would thrive throughout the decade, as the GI Bill made it easy to buy homes in suburbs that were popping up everywhere. Within those homes, modern appliances made housework easy.

Almost every household had that one appliance that changed everything by the late 1950s: television! America had a love affair with a certain daffy redhead, and women looked to iconic TV moms like June Cleaver and Harriet Nelson for fashion cues. Running a vacuum in a full-skirted shirtwaist, pearls, and heels was not unusual for a stylish housewife, who strove to please her breadwinner husband with a tidy house, trim figure, and attractive appearance.

The no-longer New Look stayed in vogue and in demand, and many women payed slavish attention to *Vogue* and other fashion magazines. Their strict rules stated, among other things, that you could wear the same suit from morning to dinner, but a lady must change to an evening bag or risk being "tsked" at the country club. For the impeccably dressed, matching gloves, shoes, and purses were essentials In some stylish families, matching mother-daughter outfits, down to purse and gloves, were ever-so-chic.

By the late '50s, teenagers emerged as rock 'n' rolled life forces of their own and demanded carefree, youthful alternatives to their mothers' stately ensembles as well as fun purses to jazz up their outfits. Purse makers bopped up their variety to tantalize teen shoppers.

Though generally smaller and sleeker than during WWII, purses ranged from uber-expensive designer leather to box purses to fun and quirky Lucite in rainbows of colors. The purse as icon flourished: Coco Chanel's black quilted-leather bag with gilt-chain handle debuted in 1955, the Hermès "Kelly Bag" in 1956, and Gucci's bamboo-handled bag in 1957. Though "the rules" dictated at least one good leather bag, many women found cheaper synthetics offered the look without the price.

Whatever the price point, any artful homemaker's bag included makeup, trading stamps, store coupons, a notepad and pencil, an address book, keys to the station wagon, cash, checks, (possibly) cigarettes, a lady's handkerchief, and, for mothers, candy and toys to entertain the kids—or bribe them to behave.

Lucite Tiered Box Purse
with gold thread confetti

Creaciones de Vicki

Leather architectural
yin and yang design
with curvaceous
one-piece handle

Margaret Ann and Carol

Little Rock, Arkansas
1950 – 1959

The new Wurlitzer Jukebox holds fifty-two records. Margaret Ann and her brother, Everett, are illuminated as they read of the 104 song selections. It's 1:30 p.m. on Monday, September 22, 1958. The Drug Store soda shop on Main Street in Little Rock, Arkansas, is crowded with teenagers. Normally, it would be a school day, but not today.

Everett: "How about playing 'Purple People Eater'?"

Margaret Ann: "With my quarter, we're listening to Elvis, Bobby Darin, and Bill Haley. You go to Moses Melody and use the listening booth."

Everett: "Play A41, 'Splish Splash.' Sis, would you buy me a cherry Coke?"

Margaret Ann looks through her sister Patricia's hand-me-down poodle purse that coordinates with her circle skirt. Usually by September, she would have a new purse, but not this year. Since the governor closed Little Rock's four high schools, her senior year is uncertain. Every family is scrambling to find schools in other locations for the 1958–59 school year. Margaret Ann's mom adamantly told her, "There'll be no family split. We live a block from Central High. I will see it reopened, and the twenty-seven teachers rehired!" Since September 1957, when national news showed their neighborhood streets filled with integration protesters, the Arkansas National Guard, and soldiers from the 101st Airborne Division, worried relatives from Georgia to California had contacted her family. Little Rock looked very dangerous.

Margaret Ann: "Here's a nickel for your Coke."

Everett: "For two pennies, I get an extra squirt of cherry."

Margaret Ann: "You're an awful beggar. I'm taking it out of the 50 cents Mom gave me for you to see *The Blob* at the Center Theater. Just don't come home talking about aliens consuming everything on Earth. Did you see Carol at Sweden Creme?"

Everett: "Yeah. She said she's going to Kempner's for shoes since she's starting at the new free school, T.J. Raney High."

Margaret Ann: "Did you see Boyd, Dick, or Jerry?"

Everett: "Nope. I saw Harry from Mabelvale with his hot rod! They call him 'J.D.'"

Margaret Ann: "Juvenile delinquent. Some people think Elvis is a 'J.D.' How silly. Music isn't dangerous like drag racing. And Harry isn't admirable, Everett."

Everett: "His car is though! Hey, I saw Dent and he's going back east to school by Trailways—thirty miles east to Hazen."

Two years prior, Margaret Ann's family purchased a home within walking distance of Central High School. It was a nice neighborhood with friendly people. Then during the 1957–58 school year, her father received an ominous warning from their neighbor: *You'd better watch your family*. The neighbor heard Margaret Ann was friendly to a black student in glee club. Everything seemed at odds now: the governor, the president, the army, the United States Supreme Court, and the neighbors.

Margaret Ann's dad supported education. His father was a high school principal in a small town with schools and neighborhoods segregated by a railroad track dividing the white side from the black. Yet, in the downtown stores, Margaret Ann could mingle with the black ladies as they all shopped, watching them try on the fancy wide-brimmed hats they'd match with velvet purses. One lady told her the peacock feather fans were for gospel tent revivals.

Over the summer, Margaret Ann anticipated the excitement of her senior year while envying her older sister. Patricia became engaged to a Fort Chaffee army medic who had watched Elvis get his famous army haircut, from pompadour to crewcut. Margaret Ann accompanied their mother to shop for Patricia's bridal trousseau. At M.M. Cohn's, they found a new sack dress, white kid gloves, and a black antelope suede purse with a gold catch fancy enough for Audrey Hepburn. Nothing was purchased for Margaret Ann's upcoming school year.

Carol *(just arriving at the jukebox)*: "Hey, Margaret Ann. Look at my new red and white Oxford shoes! I can join the dance party on *Steve's Show*! You heard I was going to T. J. Raney, right?"

Margaret Ann: "Yes. Will is going to prep school in Tennessee. Dick's parents let him join the Navy. Edie is going to Oklahoma to live with an aunt. We're all separating! I doubt I'll ever get to write a story in the school newspaper again."

Carol: "Or get to go to the biggest prom dance in Arkansas. Hey, let's get tickets to *Steve's Show*? With your circle skirt and poodle purse, you might get on camera."

Margaret Ann: "Sorry, I have to help mom. She's sending out invitations for an important ladies' meeting."

Carol: "Okay, call me tonight. Wait! I have a dime for the jukebox in my new leather coin purse! I've got to hear Ricky Nelson's 'Poor Little Fool.' He is so dreamy!"

1960s

The contented, conservative prosperity of the 1950s spilled over into the next decade, hanging around, innocuously, for the first few years. No. 1 hits in 1960, Bryan Hyland's "Itsy Bitsy Teenie Weenie Yellow Polka Dot Bikini" and Chubby Checker's "The Twist," perfectly captured the tone of those early years, when teenagers were contented just to hang loose and have fun. And their parents could agree to disagree about politics at cocktail parties or civic meetings without things getting heated.

But that was just the calm before the storm. Vietnam caused a major tear in the social fabric and the new American revolution soon shredded the decorum of the post WWII years, encompassing civil rights, women's rights, and the baby boom generation that turned its back on the stuffy rules and mores of its predecessors. The Beatles' "Revolution" in 1968 and Edwin Starr's 1969 hit "War" rang out the unrest common in the U.S. from the mid-1960s on. In some ways, the country would come apart at the seams by the end of the decade.

Fashion-wise, nothing was as decisive and divisive as the miniskirt, though pantsuits for women ran a close second. After a brief fling with acceptance during WWII, trousers for women walked back in the closet during the '50s; when they strode back out paired with jackets or matching tops as haute couture in the '60s, most women embraced them with open arms and defiantly dared anyone to force them back into dresses.

Purses in the 1960s were as diverse as political opinions and heavily influenced by the youth movement. Instead of slavishly following fashion magazines and lusting after structured designer bags, young women were persuaded by their peers, politics, and space-age technology. Purses ranged from hippie shoulder bags in India-inspired fabrics to sleek, shiny, or wet-look go-go bags. An especially swinging look was the micro-miniskirt coupled with a long shoulder bag worn diagonally across the body.

Whether paired with a pantsuit or a miniskirt, the shoulder bag kept hands free for living, loving, and catching whatever life threw a woman's way. No matter the purse style, structured or slouch, a peek inside might reveal sunglasses, a wallet, keys, cigarettes, pills (legal or not-so), hair accessories, scarves, letters from soldiers, books, even top hit singles on 45 records—and, later in the decade, life-altering, liberating birth control pills.

The '60s may have been divisive, but they were also definitive. Feminine fashions changed forever, and so did the females who wore them.

Handmade Purse
Mask design with gold embellishments

Smiley Face Purse
Patent leather

Edie Bridges and Holly Bridges

Kansas City, Missouri
1960 – 1969

It is early morning on Saturday, May 27, 1967. Edie and Holly Bridges—twins soon to be sweet sixteen—sit poolside. The cool temperature means no swimming. At home near the Verona Columns in Mission Hills, Kansas, a well-to-do suburb of Kansas City, the girls listen to the WHB-AM request show on their PortiPlay, waiting for the weekly *40 Star "Super Hit" Survey*. They are looking forward to the summer of 1967.

Holly: "Can I wear your Souper Dress just once?"

Edie: "No way! You already ironed a hole in yours. With your luck, you'll spill cola on it and you know paper dresses can't be washed. We still have two cans of Campbell's vegetable. Just send them off with a dollar and order another. I want to wear mine when Lewis comes over Monday afternoon to watch *Where the Action Is* so I'm practicing sitting without tearing it. Look, *Seventeen*'s cover story is about paper dresses!"

Holly: "Mother is just barely letting Lewis come over. She thinks he's too old. Dad doesn't like his father either—something to do with the country club. She'll never let you wear a paper dress. You'll have to wear a proper sundress like Mom's."

Edie: "Yuck. No! Remember you'll have to sit in the Florida room with us. Mother assigned you chaperone duty. Ask Paul over too. Tell him to bring records."

Holly: "Listen. Some guy just requested 'Cherish' to celebrate his 20th wedding anniversary. I didn't know anyone that old listened to WHB."

Edie: "Remember last week? A lady requested 'These Boots Are Made for Walking' to celebrate her 40th birthday. That's mother's age!"

Holly: "What do you bet the number one song is this week? I say 'Respect.' I love Aretha Franklin! The Beatles will be on the charts again soon. Their new album will be out on June 2nd and Paul reserved a copy at the record store. We should have a listening party—you and Lewis, me and Paul. The album's called *Sgt. Pepper's Lonely Hearts Club Band*, I think. Paul said WHB is having an album cover contest too."

Edie: "That's next Friday. We should use the living room stereo. You ask Mother, okay? Hey, can I trade you my paper dress for your smiley face purse?"

Holly: "No deal. But I'll loan it if you'll let me use the cat-and-owl box purse. Did you hear me playing the piano this morning? Now I can play 'Something Stupid,' and 'The Sound of Silence.' I still can't believe the Monkees performed in Wichita and not in KC."

Edie: "Lewis and his friends from Pembroke drove over to see the Monkees, but they really wanted to see the opening act, Jimi Hendrix. He plays acid rock."

Holly: "Well, don't tell mother Lewis listens to acid rock. She freaked out when Paul played that banana album in the living room and she heard the word heroin."

Edie: "Guess what? Yesterday, Lewis got a letter of acceptance to Tulane for the fall! New Orleans. I only have him for the summer—him and his metallic blue Cougar."

Holly: "Don't get ahead of yourself. They won't even allow you to see him after dark yet. Why didn't you ask him over to watch the Turtles on *American Bandstand* today?"

Edie: "Dad's at home. He doesn't much like Lewis, Mom said, because Lewis didn't wear a proper suit and tie to see our ballet recital. Good thing he doesn't know Lewis drove us home twice from ballet practice after dark."

Holly: "Paul was going through Volker Park, to that record store where he buys Charlie Parker albums, and this TV crew from CBS stopped him. He was wearing his blue jeans and white tunic shirt. They thought he was a hippie with his long hair, but they cut the filming short when Paul told them he lived in Mission Hills."

Edie: "Mother was so proud when CBS could only find a few hippies in Kansas City. I can't believe Paul is moving to Chicago. He's lived next door to us all our lives."

Holly: "Paul said he would really miss us and the record store. He told me if my improvisational skill on the piano keeps getting better, he'll come get me and we'll start a band."

Edie: "You know you couldn't have a Dior cocktail dress or a Kelly bag if you were in a rock band."

Holly: "But I don't want a cocktail dress. You're the one who wanted to try on the Givenchy evening gown from Paris. No wait, you *didn't* want to, that was —"

Edie and Holly together: *"MOTHER'S IDEA!"*

1970s

The 1970s began as a continuation of the hippie movement and ended with the reckless abandon of the dance-the-night-away disco era. But The Beatles' breakup in April 1970 in some ways set the tone for the decade: Divisions in the U.S. grew starker, Vietnam War protests grew more violent, and disillusionment with "the man" replaced optimism for change. The mid-decade Watergate scandal turned some, especially young people, into political activists, and growing concern over the environment energized others.

Women entered the workforce in unprecedented numbers, which shook up the status quo and was met with unhappy resistance from some Americans, male and female. Fashion, as usual, reflected the changes in society.

Many women tended to fall into one of two main types. Type One was the buttoned-down, put-together, well-dressed working woman (or PTA mom), with every hair in place and nary a wrinkle or rumple in her attire. Lipstick? But of course. Type Two was the free-spirited bohemian, with a hippie-chick vibe. Lip gloss? What else? Of course some women moved easily along the spectrum, depending on the occasion. Pants continued to make great strides for women's fashions; bell-bottoms blossomed into palazzo pants and pantsuits gained power. Blue jeans became ubiquitous for men and women alike, and by the end of the decade were appropriate attire for practically

anywhere. And, oh, those hot pants! In the '70s these super-short shorts, worn over tights or more-daring bare legs, were almost as common in high school halls as on the disco dance floor.

Purses ran the gamut in this decade, from in-your-face, military-style bags to mock the war to battered, unconstructed hippie bags to the sexy disco bags worn like ornaments on the dance floor. But "the" bag of the 1970s was the large, soft-leather or suede shoulder bag. Carried slung across the shoulder or body, with numerous pockets and zippers, these bags seemed to equip women for anything in the new age of feminism.

A look into a working woman's roomy bag might reveal makeup, a hairbrush, scarves, protest pamphlets, political buttons, brochures, an address book, a business card holder, and birth control (whether pills or condoms). On the flip side, a peek into a disco diva's shiny bag toward the end of the decade might reveal different essentials: money, makeup, a tiny hairbrush and, just maybe, cocaine to keep her energized.

Roberta Di Camerino
Velvet and leather

Leather Handbag
with velvet kaleidoscope pattern and turn lock closure

Daisy and Anjelica

Boulder, Colorado

1970 – 1979

September 9, 1974. Pearl Street Food King.

"Mom, will Uncle Max bring a shoulder bag for my Barbie?" Anjelica, about to begin second grade, leaned against the meat display case. "He promised to make a leather bag just like your Kaleidoscope bag, but Barbie-sized!"

"Honey, Uncle Max and Uncle Freddie are just having dinner with us tonight. We'll go to his leather shop tomorrow and get Barbie a bag," Daisy said to her daughter. They were at the store to buy ingredients for Julia Child's quiche recipe: spinach, shallots, Swiss cheese, a pastry shell, and eggs. Daisy had only stopped rolling her cart briefly, so she could accept a free slice of pizza from an aproned lady. Her work as a women's health care counselor-in-training at the Boulder Free Clinic didn't allow her time for lunch, due to the recent influx of young, idealistic "bohemians" into the city. She was also working toward a certificate in public health. With such demands on her time, her last "date night" with her husband Oliver had been five months ago, when Joni Mitchell played the Balch Fieldhouse.

Daisy's job was to evaluate individuals for free care. Earlier in the day, she had gone to check up on a group of free-spirited women living in buses in the mountains. In addition to inviting Daisy to their local music jam, they asked questions about birth control, prenatal care, and infant vaccinations.

"Mommy . . . dog food," said Yuri, aged 3, as he dropped a piece of his apple onto the supermarket floor, like he always did at home for their dog Benji. They lived in the guest house next to Daisy's mother's home, just off South Boulder Road.

Daisy's mother, Nora Ruth, known as "Roo," took care of Yuri and Angelica until 5 o'clock on weekdays, and then attended night classes at the new Naropa University, where "Buddhism-meets-great-Western-thought" was the school motto. Besides attending school and helping take care of her grandchildren, Roo also volunteered with organizations that promoted clean water and historic preservation.

"Yuri," Daisy said calmly, "Benji isn't here to eat the apple. We'll go home soon and I'll make you some mashed potatoes with alfalfa."

"Mom," Anjelica interjected, "I need a lunch box for school! Could I get a Benji one?"

"You and Roo are going to make a lunchbox," Daisy reminded her.

Anjelica had been born the year Daisy and Oliver graduated from the University of Colorado. Yuri arrived four years later. Oliver was from Bridgeport, Connecticut, and had been lucky to receive a high number in the draft lottery. As a freshman English major, he'd spent more time rock climbing than doing school work. Daisy, who'd grown up in Boulder, met Oliver on a geology field trip to the Flatiron Cliffs. Their first date was for hamburgers at The Sink, and they'd seldom been apart since.

The local radio station KOAQ was playing on the supermarket intercom. After Eric Clapton's "I Shot the Sheriff" ended, the station played its singsong call letters "KOAQ, Q-1-0-3!" and segued into a news announcement preceded by the sound of a teletype machine.

Just then Anjelica began singing: "A man and a woman had a little baby, yes, they did, they had three in the family, that's a magic number." Yuri kicked his Birkenstocks rhythmically in response, while Daisy tried to listen to the radio. "This is the complete replay of yesterday's stunning announcement," the reporter said before playing a recording: "Now, therefore, I, Gerald R. Ford, President of the United States, pursuant to the pardon power conferred upon me by Article II, Section 2, of the Constitution, have granted and by these presents do grant a full, free, and absolute pardon unto Richard Nixon . . ."

Daisy immediately thought of Oliver's job reporting news at the local, low-power, daytime-only public radio station, where the Nixon pardon was no doubt being discussed in depth. What Daisy wanted to hear, though, was what Max, Freddie, and Oliver would have to say that night. Max was an attorney and leather craftsman. Freddie had served with the 101st Airborne Division in Vietnam, and was about to receive a bachelor's degree in geology courtesy of the GI Bill. Oliver, to help write his news reports, read everything he could. What they all had in common was the love of serious, fact-based debate.

Daisy anticipated Max pulling books, magazines, and maps out of his handmade messenger bag. Freddie would bring an assortment of newspapers in his monogrammed leather shoulder bag. Oliver and Daisy would serve the meal and participate as equals in the informed and emotional discussions of the so-far very eventful 1970s.

1980s

The 1980s ushered in a whole new dynamic as video killed the radio star, young people stayed home to watch their MTV, and Ronald Reagan, the actor turned politician, was elected president. Twice. Women stepped into the role of '80s superwoman and super-mom, the empowered woman with big shoulder pads who could have it all: beautiful appearance, lovely home, enviable figure, well-mannered kids, and powerful career.

Higher wages and dual incomes gave rise to status dressing in designer clothes for all ages, with the designer's logo prominently displayed. Even toddlers were logo-ed. "Yuppies" (young, upwardly mobile professionals) poked fun at hippies and yippies of yore, as the in-phrase of the tax-cutting '80s became "greed is good," via the hit movie *Wall Street*. Joan Collins' over-the-top Alexis Carrington of the '80s TV smash *Dynasty* was the embodiment of that decree and the power suit.

As consumerism ruled the day, fitness became a national obsession; buff bodies were a status symbol in their own right, and women thought nothing of shopping and running errands in Spandex exercise attire or sportswear which might include leotards and leg warmers. The "preppie" look embodied casual wear, but women in offices took the power suit to a new degree of ferocity

with vibrant colors, short, tight skirts, and oversize shoulder pads, paired with bold jewelry and large designer bags. The super-busy '80s superwoman relied ever more on her purse: Having it all often meant carrying it all.

Whether high-quality leather or rubberized cotton, a purse in the 1980s was packed with wallet, keys, coupons, sunglasses, eyeglasses, and makeup, as well as paperwork, business cards, a calculator, and calendar, along with a low-calorie lunch to eat at a desk and athletic shoes to wear to and from the office. A working mother's bag would also feature disposable diapers, toys, and a magazine or book to read while the kids practiced soccer or took dance lessons.

Logo-adorned designer purses achieved cult status in the 1980s, and purses were advertised as not only vital accessories but lust-worthy items. A woman's very sanity depended on a well-packed purse.

Morris Moskowitz
Snakeskin hobo bag

Large Round Shoulder Bag

Leather with chrome accents

Phyllis, Patricia, Hazel, and Alice

Las Vegas, Nevada
1980 – 1989

In Las Vegas, on April 21, 1984, the Saturday before Easter, four friends are playing bridge. They are middle-aged, have no family members living within a thousand miles, and all recently moved to the Summerlin community, "a quiet oasis" within a rapidly growing city. The bridge club that meets in the neighborhood commons helps heal their homesickness. Phyllis with the chunky gold necklace, Hazel with the turquoise ring, and their bridge partners, Alice and Patricia, sit in a cool corner under a bamboo ceiling fan.

"I moved here because I loved Vegas," Patricia says. "Back in the '70s, I saw Sonny and Cher at the Sahara and won at the blackjack table at the Sands. For us Hawaiians, Vegas is considered the ninth Hawaiian island." She focuses on her cards. "1 No Trump."

"Patricia and I and our future ex-husbands vacationed here together," Alice reminisces. "After we both got divorced and I retired from teaching fourth graders we found affordable Vegas homes near two malls and a country club. It's been great, except the heat may break me. I miss the lush green and moderate temperatures of Hawaii. The holidays always make me think of *ohana*, the family in Hawaii." After taking a drink of iced tea Alice says, "2 clubs."

Phyllis says, "I think the heat is a surprise to us all. Who dealt these cards? Oh my, I forgot! I did! 2 hearts."

Hazel waits a moment, and takes a serious tone, "7 spades."

"7 spades!" Phyllis laughs. "You kidding? Wait—that's the crazy bid from that movie we watched the other night, *Grand Slam* with Loretta Young. She had a TV show, too, where she opened her living room doors and swirled around in the latest designer gown. Remember?"

"3 hearts," says Hazel. "One thing Las Vegas has is shopping. I know a shop in Fashion Show Mall with imitation clothes, hats, and purses based on Hollywood and TV show wardrobes. I saw a copy of the dress Shirley MacLaine wore in *Terms of Endearment*. It was chiffon with a large floral print." Hazel's eyes glow with excitement.

"6 diamonds," says Alice. "Good play, partner. The dummy puts down the dummy." She pauses a second, then says, "I wonder if they have that two-piece gown Miss Ellie wore to the Oil Barons' Ball. It was perfect. Phyllis, is your lovely purse a Gucci satin clutch?"

"It's a Sharif design made of tapestry, from Neiman Marcus. I found it on sale! I shop almost every day since Henry's always at the Convention Center. He covered that huge Consumer Electronics Show and wrote an article about a home computer with a screen as colorful as a TV set. I think we should go to that leather shop at Boulevard Mall. Who needs an Easter bonnet when you can get a cherry red leather purse? But I'm a little scared since that mall sales clerk was kidnapped." Phillis lets Alice take a closer look at her purse, then says, "Pass."

Patricia, speaking to Hazel, says, "Your husband works on the Strip. How's it going down there? Pass." The table's attention turns to Hazel.

"Pretty bad. There's been something like a 70% decline at the casinos. 17,000 workers on strike since April 2nd and that includes food service, bartenders, musicians, and stagehands. It's even slowing down construction plans." Hazel gives a heavy sigh. "4 down double."

"The strike just has to end soon. My son, John, is coming from Chicago to see the Grateful Dead band. Can you imagine a hippie band at the Aladdin? No suits and ties—only tie dye!" Phyllis giggles. "End of game. 1,400 points."

"Cut the deck and let's pick," Alice says. "Now, who watched *Dallas* last night? Didn't you feel sorry for Katherine Wentworth after J.R. tried blackmailing her with the video?"

"I did," Hazel says. "I mean J.R. took a secret video of Katherine in bed with him! And he's going to show Bobby! There may be another end-of-season shooting." She leans in and says, "I hope Bobby and Pam get back together."

Phyllis says quickly, "Well, I hope no one messes up Miss Ellie getting married. At her age, she deserves a good man!" She offers the deck to each to choose a card.

"High card, I deal," says Patricia. "I've always liked the daytime dramas myself. I just saw Neil and Liz's wedding on *Days of Our Lives*. Don't you all feel our days do seem to pass 'like sand through an hourglass'?"

1990s

As Americans grew weary of the excesses of the '80s, the plaid-coated and gravelly-voiced grunge scene out of Seattle grew to prominence in the early 1990s. Nirvana and Pearl Jam shook things up, while a couple of rising political stars from the South gained acclaim (and the presidency and vice presidency) by taking stands for the poor, the environment, and global consciousness. By mid-decade, political differences were more divisive than ever, but almost everyone agreed that the ugly fashion extremes of the previous decade had to go.

The grunge influence on young people and a backlash against '80s power dressing in general turned down the volume on fashion once again, and teens (and others) raided their fathers' closets and thrift stores for tattered denim and frayed flannel. Those who embraced couture were dubbed "fashionistas," which could be a compliment or a slur, depending on the source. Basing one's life on fashion excess was *Clueless*, as exemplified by the Alicia Silverstone teen hit movie.

The 1990s nodded to androgyny with flannel shirts and Converse shoes for all in the early years. For working women, slimmer tailored skirts or pantsuits were back. Men and women also dabbled with unisex fashion in the form of khakis—every mall had at least one store that carried them—and jeans became more popular than ever as stores and designers offered a cut for every body type. New

"mom" jeans meant even postpartum women could be comfortable. Backpacks were carried by virtually everyone in the early '90s, from junior high boys to busy moms. Unisex fragrances like CK One could be shared by sisters and brothers, girlfriends and boyfriends.

As the decade progressed, "good" feminine accessories made a comeback, and women tended to spend more on designer bags than they'd spend on clothes. Dress styles would come and go, but a sturdy leather purse by Dooney & Bourke made a statement and would last for years. A return to smaller, softer shapes brought femininity back to handbags, but short-strap bags, held over the arm and close to the body in a feminine stance, grew larger as the '90s progressed, in part because women had more to carry than ever.

Whether a woman carried a small, neatly packed purse or giant bag, the contents would include the classics—wallet, keys, makeup, hairbrush, glasses, and sunglasses—proving some things never change. But now, added to the mix were assorted technological gadgets: pager, PDA, cell phone, water bottle, flat iron or curling iron, and later in the decade even a laptop computer.

Chanel
Quilted lambskin
shoulder bag

Paloma Picasso
Black calfskin with diamond embellishments

Roxanne, Gracie, Paula, and Jane

San Francisco, California
1990 – 1999

Roxanne, the youngest of the three Weir daughters, admired her older sisters, Gracie and Paula. While Gracie was successful in business and Paula in medicine, Roxanne had married at eighteen and become a single mother by age twenty. Her daughter Jane, now twenty-five, had decided to have an early Christmas party for the sisters and herself. The women gathered at the Weir family home in the Mission District, a Victorian-era house that had sheltered four generations and survived the 1906 San Francisco earthquake and fire. Roxanne, now working as a bank branch manager, lives in the house with her parents and Jane.

Roxanne opened the first present. "Gracie!" she exclaimed. "This is your 1983 Gucci purse! I remember it—you bought it when you worked in advertising at the winery! You said Gucci was real style in the face of kitsch."

"Merry Christmas, Roxanne," Gracie replied with a satisfied smile. "Jane said you looked for this type of Gucci bag in several vintage stores. So here is your own blue-and-red Boston doctor bag with monogrammed logo, along with some of my travel souvenirs."

"I see! Some soap from the Hotel George V in Paris, and postcards of the Berlin Wall and Disneyland." Roxanne pulled out a London Underground map and added, "Could you please help Jane plan a honeymoon?" Gracie, the oldest sister, was the family's expert traveler.

Paula was a nurse caring for HIV/AIDS cases at San Francisco General Hospital. To relax, she liked to shop and watch *Seinfeld*. "Have you seen the new 1993 Gucci bags?" she asked. "I. Magnin has a miniature purse and a slouch bag in gold leather displayed in their jewelry window."

Jane, a costume apprentice with the San Francisco Opera, silently observed the fashion differences between the women. "Aunt Gracie," she said, "when I make journeyman, Lloyd and I want to take our honeymoon." Roxanne at that moment dumped the contents of her woven tote onto the table, causing Jane to exclaim, "Mom, you can't put all that in your Gucci bag!"

Her Aunt Paula wore blended materials, always ivory or cream, with jackets. Her mother dressed in colorful cottons or linens. Her Aunt Gracie was almost always wearing black silk with expensive accessories.

"What do we have here?" Roxanne said with mock surprise. "My wallet, address book, compact, lipstick, Kleenex, box of Christmas cards, Walkman, scrunchie, *Schindler's List* in paperback, perfume, nail polish, matches." Holding up a woman's watch she asked herself, "Does this even work?"

"Roxanne, I bet you could find another purse in that tote," Gracie said dryly.

Jane spoke up. "Mom, I want to take a photo to remember today, December 20th, 1993. When I hit the timer, we have ten seconds. You guys stand up, shoulder to shoulder, and I'll jump in. Okay, look at the Nikon and stand up straight. Think *Vogue*." The camera shutter clicked.

After three more photos, they all relaxed in the den. Paula stretched out on the chaise lounge and said, "Jane, I hear you'll be with Lloyd and his parents on Christmas. I'm glad you found him. It's dangerous to date around right now."

Gracie got to the point and asked, "Does Lloyd have a job? Do you have a picture of him?"

"Well, I have this photo-booth photo," Jane said, smiling with apparent pride. "He has long blond hair, like Brad Pitt. He's from a military family in Bellingham, Washington, and works in stage lighting, even though he's educated in computer programming. He worked on lighting for *Mrs. Doubtfire*, and I met him at a wrap party for the movie in July. Our wedding will be on April 8. We want a family wedding here in grandmother's garden with a Catholic priest and a Presbyterian minister. Then Lloyd and I are going to Seattle for the weekend." She touched her engagement ring engraved with Celtic symbols. "And, Aunt Paula, we got our HIV tests. Lloyd didn't mind it."

Jane paused briefly, then continued, "The head costume designer at work found a vintage 1950s wedding dress for me. He said I have a nice Leslie Caron figure, but it usually doesn't show because of my baggy clothes. The gown is blush-colored taffeta with a circle skirt and petticoats. And I'm making a satin wedding handbag."

"It'll be an odd Christmas Day without you," Paula said to Jane. "Will you be here for the traditional Christmas Eve in Union Square? We must see this year's decorated store windows, and I hear the carolers are fabulous."

"Yes, and I want us to shop together every Christmas Eve into the 21st century!" Jane said excitedly. "I'll always want to see the handbags at I. Magnin. And this year we can toast to Christmas, New Year's, Lloyd, and fabulous purses!"

SOURCES

BOOKS

Albrechtsen, Nicky. *Vintage Fashion Complete: Women's Style in the Twentieth Century*. Chronicle Books, 2014.

Baudot, Francois. *Fashion: The Twentieth Century*. Universe, 2006.

Berkson, Janice. *Carry Me: 1950's Lucite Handbags: An American Fashion*. Antique Collectors Club, 2009.

Blum, Stella. *Everyday Fashions of the Thirties As Pictured in Sears Catalogs*. Dover Publications, 1986.

Blythe, Daniel. *Collecting Gadgets and Games from the 1950s-90s*. Pen and Sword, 2011.

Bowd, Emma. *Mad about Bags*. Ryland, Peters & Small, 2002.

Burns, Bree. *America in the 1970s (Decades of American History)*. Facts on File, 2005.

Callan, Jim. *America in the 1900s and 1910s (Decades of American History)*. Facts on File, 2005.

Callan, Jim. *America in the 1930s (Decades of American History)*. Facts on File, 2005.

Callan, Jim. *America in the 1960s (Decades of American History)*. Facts on File, 2005.

Camardella, Michele L. *America in the 1980s (Decades of American History)*. Facts on File, 2005.

Corey, Melinda. *Chronology of 20th-Century America, Decades of American History*. Facts on File. 2005. 10 vols.

Cox, Caroline. *The Handbag: An Illustrated History*. HarperCollins, 2007.

Dooner, Kate. *Plastic Handbags: Sculpture to Wear*. Schiffer Publishing, Ltd., 2005.

Ettinger, Roseann. *Handbags*. Schiffer Publishing Ltd., 1999.

Fogg, Marnie. *Vintage Handbags*. Carlton Books Ltd., 2013.

Gallagher, Winifred. *It's in the Bag: What Purses Reveal - and Conceal*. HarperCollins, 2006.

Gottlieb, Robert, et al. *A Certain Style: The Art of the Plastic Handbag*. Knopf, 1988.

Grafton, Carol Belanger. *Shoes, Hats and Fashion Accessories: A Pictorial Archive, 1850-1940*. Dover Publications, 1998.

Hagerty, Barbara G. S. and Anne Rivers Siddons. *Handbags: A Peek Inside a Woman's Most Trusted Accessory*. Running Press, 2002.

Hanson, Erica. *A Cultural History of the United States Through the Decades - The 1920s*. Lucent Books, 1998.

Holiner, Richard. *Antique Purses: A History, Identification, and Value Guide*. Collector Books, 1987.

Holland, Gini. *A Cultural History of the United States Through the Decades - The 1960s*. Lucent Books, 1998.

Ivo, Sigrid. *Bags*. Pepin Press, 2011.

Johnson, Anna. *Handbags: The Power of the Purse*. Workman Publishing Company, 2002.

Kallen, Stuart A. *A Cultural History of the United States Through the Decades - The 1950s*. Lucent Books, 1998.

Kallen, Stuart A. *A Cultural History of the United States Through the Decades - The 1980s*. Lucent Books, 1998.

Kallen, Stuart A. *A Cultural History of the United States Through the Decades - The 1990s*. Lucent Books, 1998.

Mendes, Valerie and Amy de la Haye. *Fashion Since 1900*. Thames and Hudson, 2010.

Ochoa, George. *America in the 1990s (Decades of American History)*. Facts on File, 2005.

O'Neal, Michael J. *America in the 1920s (Decades of American History)*. Facts on File, 2005.

Peacock, John. *The Complete Fashion Sourcebook*. Thames & Hudson, 2006.

Piña, Leslie, and Donald-Brian Johnson. *Popular Purses: It's in the Bag!* Schiffer Publishing Ltd., 2001.

Press, Petra. *A Cultural History of the United States Through the Decades - The 1930s*. Lucent Books, 1998.

Przybyszewski, Linda. *The Lost Art of Dress: The Women Who Once Made America Stylish*. Basic Books, 2014.

Rogers, Agnes. *Women Are Here to Stay: The Durable Sex in its Infinite Variety Through Half a Century of American Life*. Harper, 1949.

Schwartz, Lynell K. *Vintage Purses at Their Best*. Schiffer Publishing Ltd., 1995.

Silver, Cameron. *Decades: A Century of Fashion*. Bloomsbury USA, 2012.

Steele, Valerie and Laird Borrelli. *Handbags: A Lexicon of Style*. Rizzoli, 2000.

Stewart, Gail. *A Cultural History of the United States Through the Decades - The 1970s*. Lucent Books, 1998.

Steele, Valerie and Laird Borrelli. *Bags: A Lexicon of Style*. Scriptum Editions, 1999.

Twist, Clint. *The 1970s (Take Ten Years)*. Evans Brothers Ltd., 1992

Uschan, Michael V. *A Cultural History of the United States Through the Decades - The 1910s*. Lucent Books, 1998.

Uschan, Michael V. *A Cultural History of the United States Through the Decades - The 1940s*. Lucent Books, 1998.

Varricchio, Carmen. *Collectible Doll Fashions: 1970s*. Schiffer Publishing, Ltd., 2003.

Watson, Linda. *20th Century Fashion: 100 Years of Style by Decade and Designer, in Association with Vogue*. Firefly Books, Ltd, 2004.

Wilcox, Claire. *A Century of Bags: Icons of Style in the 20th Century*. Prospero, 1998.

Wilcox, Claire. *Bags*. V&A, 1999.

Wills, Charles A. *America in the 1940s (Decades of American History)*. Facts on File, 2005.

Wills, Charles A. *America in the 1950s (Decades of American History)*. Facts on File, 2005.

Woog, Adam. *A Cultural History of the United States Through the Decades - The 1900s*. Lucent Books, 1998.

SOURCES

INTERVIEWS

Frankenstein, Laura. Personal Interview. March – August 2018.

Harrison, Eric. Personal interview. July 2018.

Mize, Barbara J. Personal interview. May 2018.

Moses, Jimmy. Personal interview. June 2018.

Neal, Bryant Jerome. Personal interview. July 2018.

Norton, Andrew D. Personal interview. July 2018.

Scott, Chris. Personal interview. August 2018.

Strauss, Susan. Personal interview. August 2018.

Syphax, Fred. Personal interview. July – August 2018.

Ryan, Patricia. Personal interview. July – August 2018.

Wilson, Carol. Personal interview. June 2018.

WEB

Dirks, Tim. "The Greatest Films—by Year." *Filmsite*, AMC Networks.

"A Brief History of St. Louis." *City of St. Louis*. www.stlouis-mo.gov/visit-play/stlouis-history.cfm

Boissoneault, Lorraine. "The Original Women's March on Washington and the Suffragists Who Paved the Way." *Smithsonian*, 21 January 2017. www.smithsonianmag.com/history/original-womens-march-washington-and-suffragists-who-paved-way-180961869/

Bear, Carson. "Little Rock, Arkansas, Addresses Complex History in More Ways Than One." *National Trust for Historic Preservation*, 24 August 2018. savingplaces.org/stories/little-rock-arkansas-addresses-complex-history-in-more-ways-than-one#.W57c-GaZO9Z

Historical Society of Washington, D.C. The Historical Society of Washington, D.C. www.dchistory.org

Historic Kansas City. Historic Kansas City. www.historickansascity.org

"History of Boulder." *City of Boulder*. bouldercolorado.gov/visitors/history

"Kansas City History." *City of Kansas City*. kcmo.gov/kansas-city-history/

Mai, Lina. "'I Had a Right to Be at Central': Remembering Little Rock's Integration Battle." *TIME*, 22 September 2017. time.com/4948704/little-rock-nine-anniversary/

Maryland Historical Society. Maryland Historical Society. www.mdhs.org

Montgomery, Rick. "'Summer of Love' in Kansas City: Handfuls of hippies, a whole lot of squares." *The Kansas City Star*, 2 June 2017. www.kansascity.com/news/local/article153894614.html

"Our Historical City." *City of Little Rock*. www.littlerock.gov/city-administration/cityclerksoffice/our-historical-city/

CONTRIBUTORS

ANITA DAVIS

Anita Davis is a native Arkansan and lifelong collector who loves outsider art, Gladys Knight, dream work, her two daughters, and learning about the mysteries of life. Her varied life experience includes owning a mail-order catalog called *Pure and Simple* in the 1980s and co-owning Vagabonds coffee house and vintage store in 1990s. She has a talent for finding valuables ("They're valuable to me!") in unexpected places and has led the revitalization of Little Rock's SoMa neighborhood in which ESSE Museum & Store is located. *What's Inside* is an extension of her endeavor to explore concepts of art, history, and the feminine at ESSE—the only purse museum in the United States and one of only three in the world.

BETSY DAVIS

Having made her life her work, Betsy Davis is continually trying to find ways of connecting with the world around her. One way she achieves this is through her illustrations, such as those featured in *What's Inside*. Narrative, humor, and compassion are themes she returns to again and again. She currently resides in Santa Fe, New Mexico, with her transgender cat, Lilipants. She is a graduate of St. John's College.

GEORGE CHAMBERS

George Chambers is a Little Rock-based photographer whose lens turns from landscapes to the beautiful shapes and forms inherent in fine art and objects. Over several years, he has worked with Anita Davis and Rita Henry to photograph hundreds of purses that are part of the collection of ESSE Museum & Store as well as the private collection of Anita Davis.

LAURA CARTWRIGHT HARDY

Laura Cartwright Hardy spent her full-time career alternating between teaching high school students to write and working as a journalist at the *Arkansas Democrat-Gazette*. Today, Laura is an occasional freelance writer and constant community activist. She found great joy in helping launch ESSE Museum & Store and her writing is featured in *What's Inside* as well as on the museum's display cases.

RITA HENRY

Born in Dermott, Arkansas, Rita Henry studied creative writing at Hendrix College, where she received a B.A. in Theater Arts. During her work in advertising, teaching, photography, and historic restoration/research, she found writing to be her natural path to expressing both evidence and emotion. The *What's Inside* project involved her special areas of interest: visual art, storytelling, and women's purses.

BRANDON MARKIN

Brandon Markin is a lifelong Arkansas resident based in North Little Rock whose interests are documentary photography, photojournalism, and portraiture. His images have been published in local and international publications, as well as local group shows and galleries. Visit him at brandonmarkin.com.

NANCY NOLAN

Based in Little Rock, Nancy Nolan's commercial, interior, and art photography has been featured in *Luxe*, *House Beautiful*, *Essence*, *Traditional Home*, *Southern Living*, *Oxford American*, and elsewhere, as well as in seven books. Visit her at nnphoto.co.

STEVEN OTIS

Steven Otis studied visual communications and illustration at the Art Institute of Seattle, and has worked in advertising and at magazines including the *Oxford American* and *Little Rock Soirée*. For nearly a decade, he has worked with Anita Davis on a variety of projects related to her vision for the revitalization of Little Rock's South Main Street district.

ERIN WOOD

Erin Wood is director at Et Alia Press, and a freelance writer and editor. Her *Women Makers of Arkansas* project, featuring 50+ women creatives including Anita Davis, is forthcoming spring 2019. Her work has appeared in *Catapult*, *The Rumpus*, *Ms. Magazine's* Blog, *Psychology Today*, and elsewhere, and has been a notable in *The Best American Essays*. Visit her at woodwritingandediting.com and etaliapress.com.

www.ingramcontent.com/pod-product-compliance
Lightning Source LLC
Chambersburg PA
CBHW041530220426
43671CB00003B/44